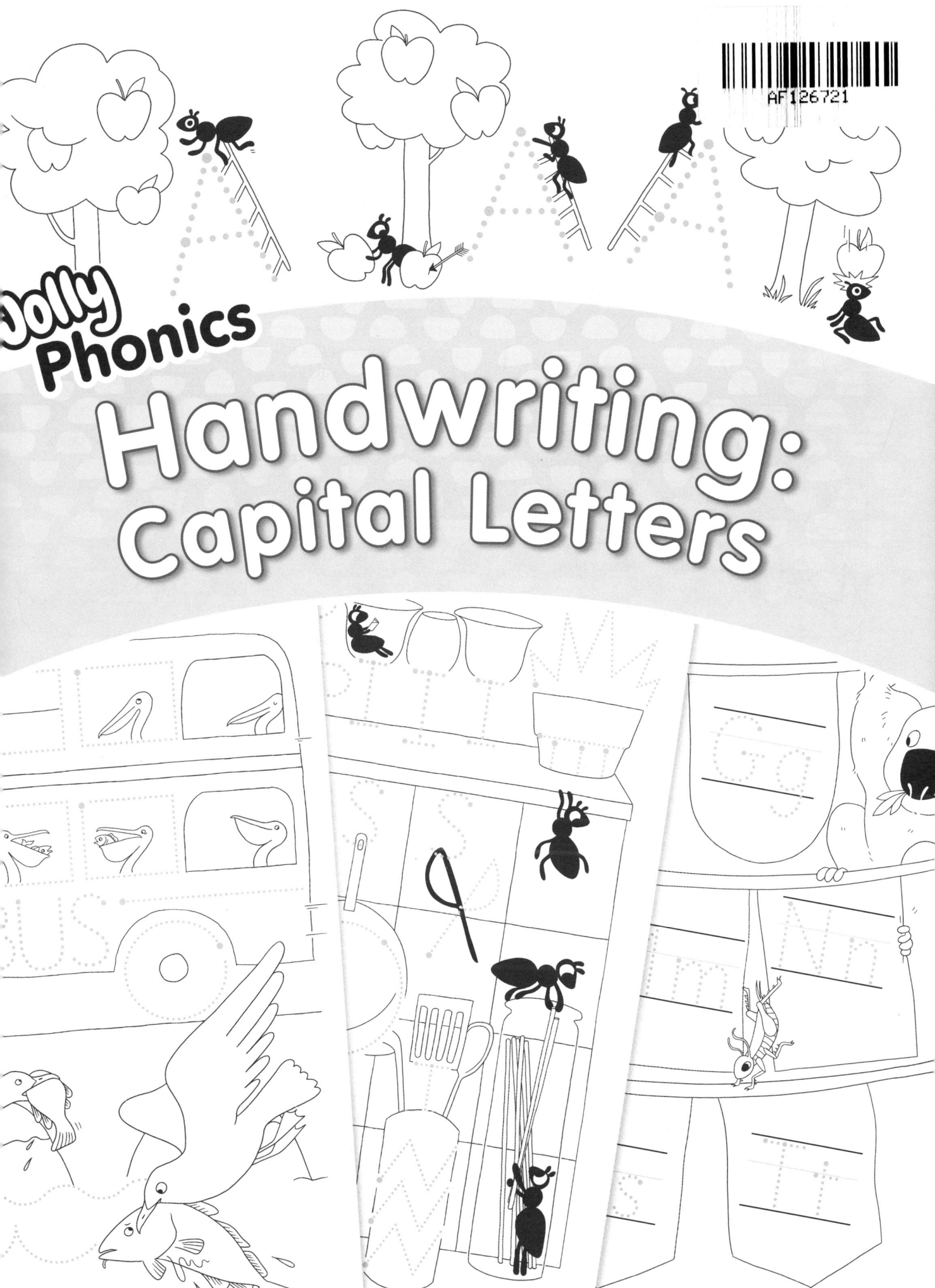

Guidelines

Good pencil control and correct formation (including knowing how to start and finish each letter) enable children to achieve neat, fluent and, eventually, joined handwriting.

Handwriting practice works best when the children are sitting at their table or desk. This provides a firm, flat surface to write on and encourages correct posture.

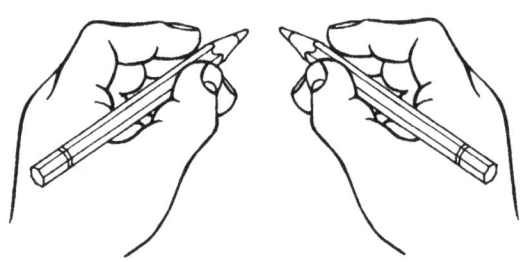

A good pencil hold from the very beginning is extremely important for developing neat, fluent handwriting. The tripod pencil hold is recommended.

Hold the pencil between the thumb and index finger, and support it on the middle finger. As the pencil is moved, the knuckles on the thumb and index finger look like a frog's legs.

Colouring is also a good way to develop fine motor skills. Encourage the children to colour carefully, to keep within the lines and to choose appropriate colours.

Spot the frog
Encourage the children to look out for the frog throughout this book, to remind them to practise their 'froggy-leg' grip.

Icon key

 Draw/trace the lines/colour

 Talk about the picture

 Look closer

Write your name in the flag and complete the castle.

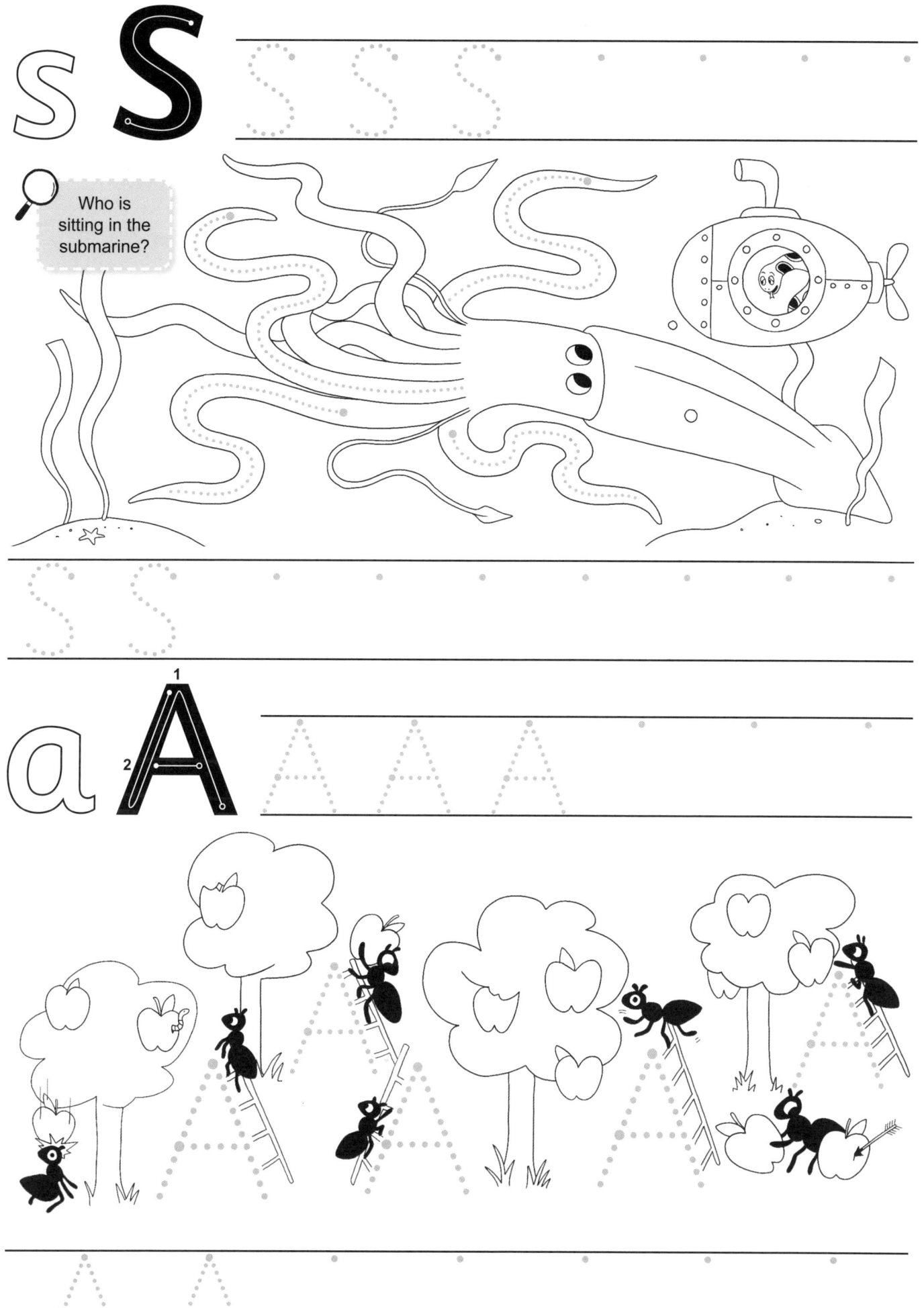

Help the parrot complete the patterns.

Which bowls have something beginning with /n/ in them?

Find out which envelope goes to which door by matching the capital and lower-case letters.

? Can you walk like a crab and click your claws like castanets?

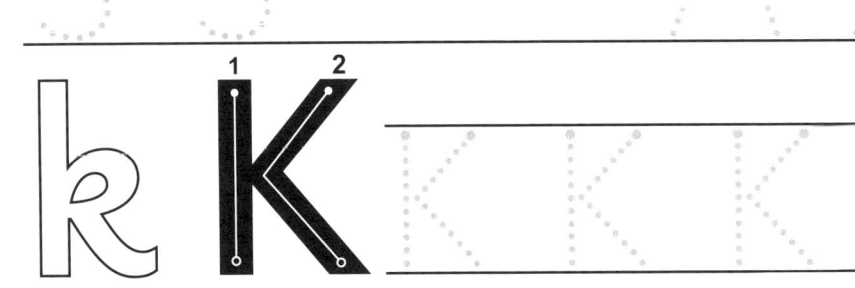

r R

Colour the rainbow. How many colours have the /r/ sound in them?

m M

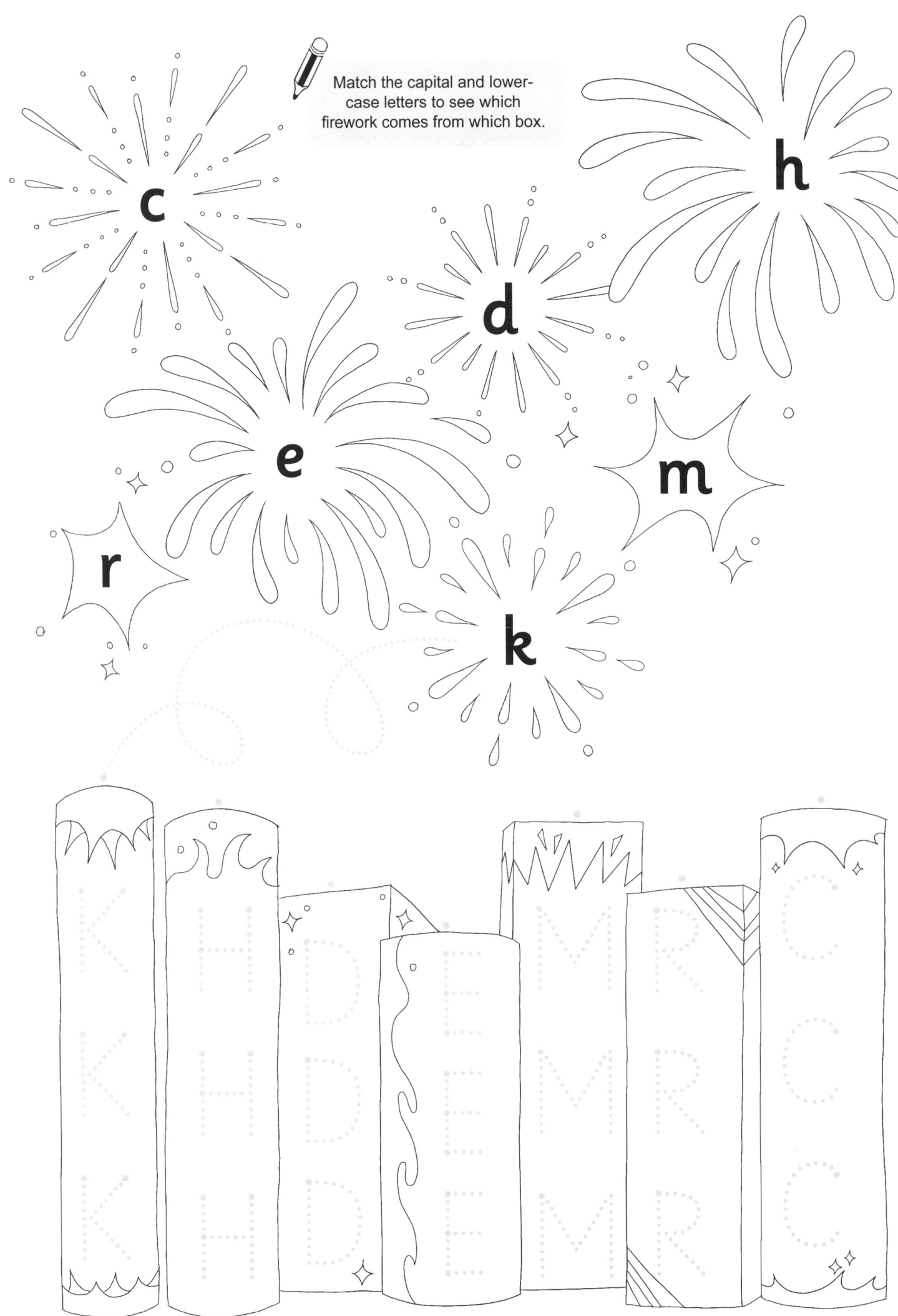

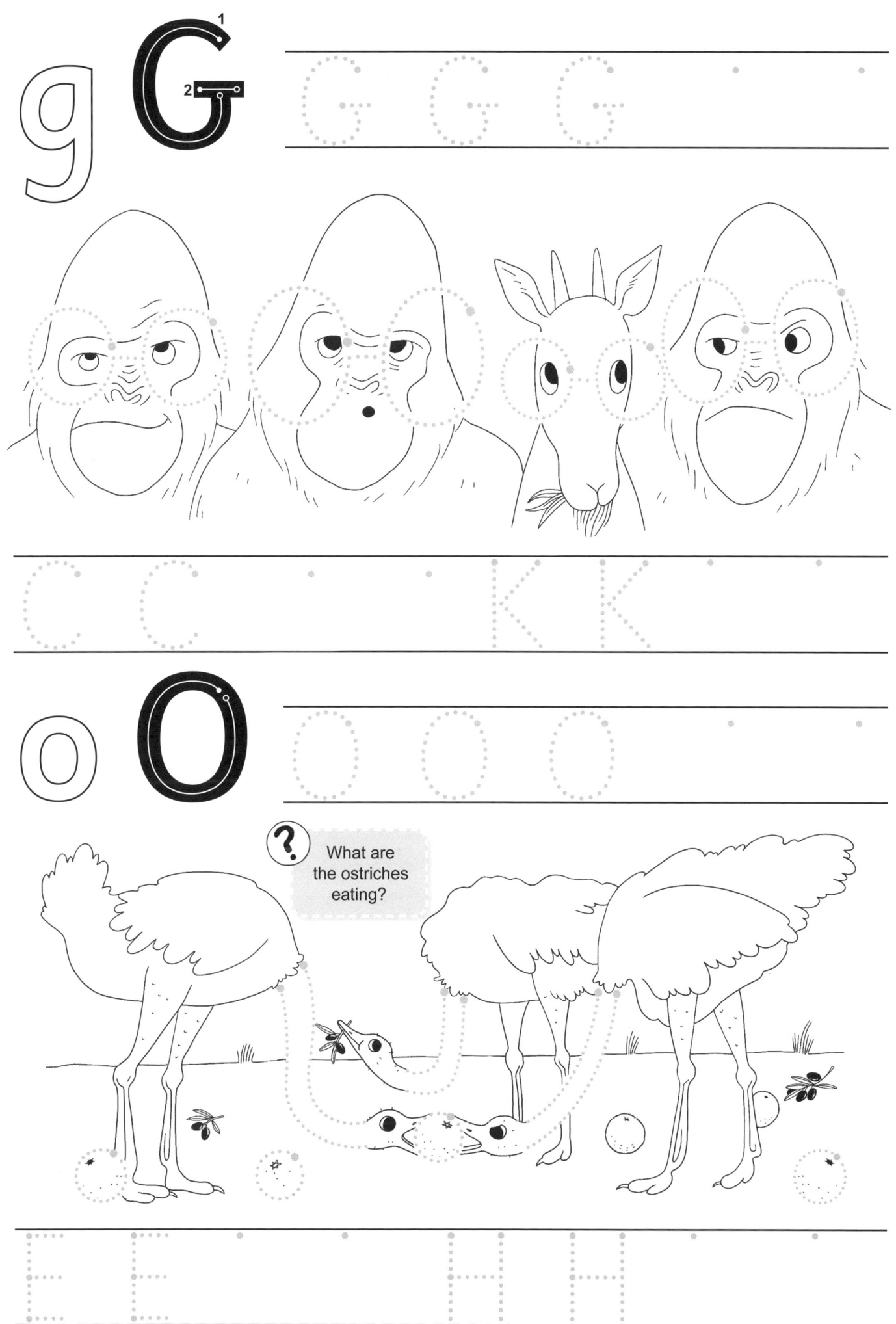

u U

l L

14

Ten pelicans sit
on a bus

Ten pelicans eat

Find out which rocket is going to which planet by matching the capital and lower-case letters.

j J

? How many of your clothes have zips on them?

z Z

18

y Y

x X

Help the fox fix the rug.

How many foxes can you count?

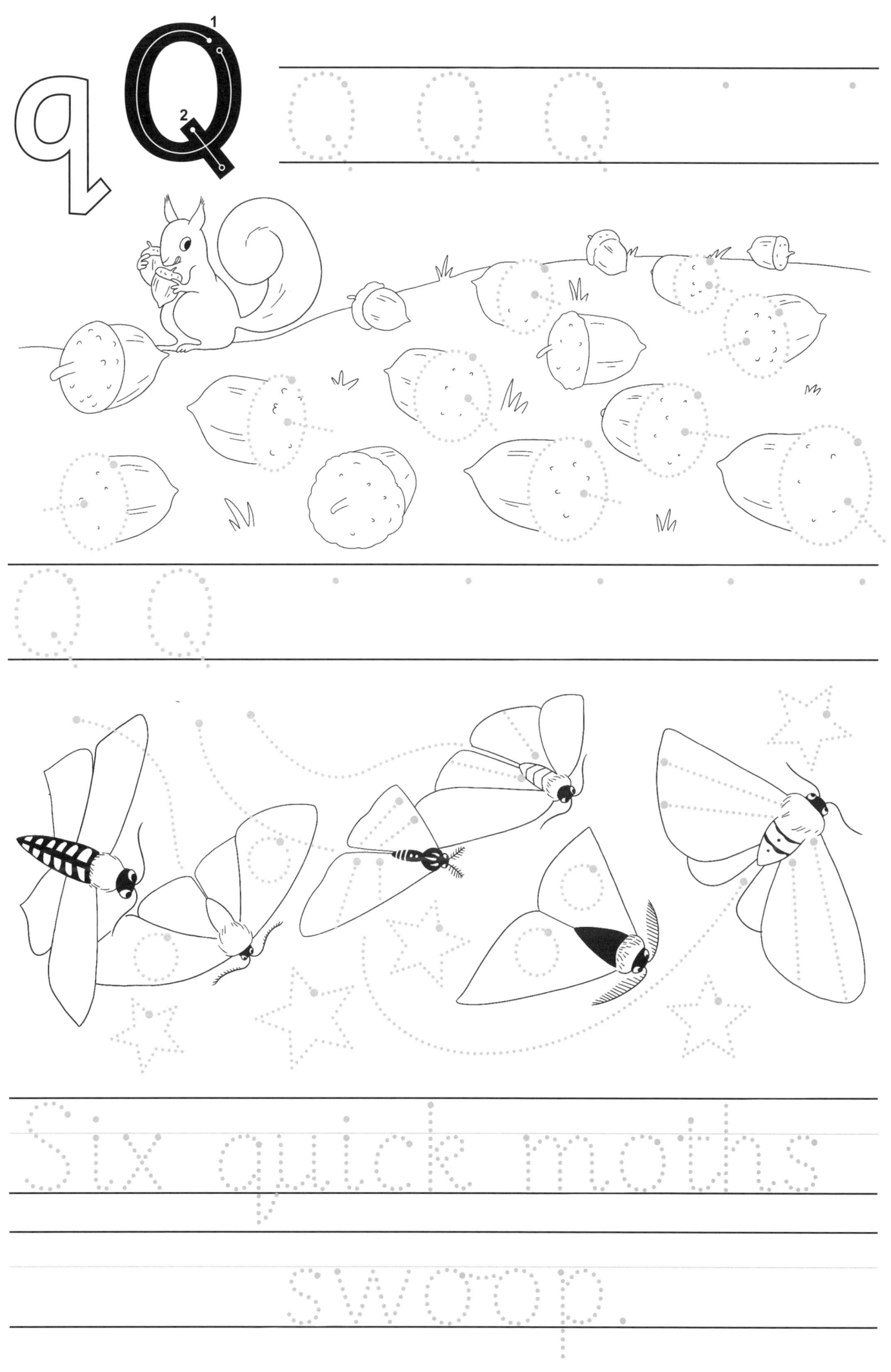

Write the letters of the alphabet.

Ages 4+

Jolly Phonics Handwriting: Capital Letters

Perfect for practising capital letter formation

This book provides letter formation practice for beginner writers. It focuses on the capital letters taught in Step 2 and includes upper- and lower-case matching activities to reinforce the link between the capitals and their letter sounds. Dotted letters and words (with starting dots) remind children how the letters are formed, and encourage them to write words using the letter sounds they know. Each page features fun activities to complete and attractive pictures to colour, which help the children to develop fine motor control.

Other books in the series:
Seven books covering the letter-sound groups taught in Step 1.

Jolly Phonics

To see the full range of Jolly Phonics products, visit our website at www.jollylearning.co.uk

© Jolly Learning 2025 (text)
© Jolly Learning 2025 (illustrations) Illustrated by Jeni Windall

77 Hornbeam Road, Buckhurst Hill, Essex,
IG9 6JX, UK. Tel: +44 20 8501 0405
82 Winter Sport Lane, Williston,
VT 05495, USA. Tel: +1-800-488-2665

Printed in the United Kingdom. All rights reserved.

www.jollylearning.co.uk   info@jollylearning.co.uk

FSC MIX Paper | Supporting responsible forestry
FSC® C023471

ISBN 978-1-83582-275-3

Reference: JL2753